Why do we have?

DAY AND NIGHT

By Claire Llewellyn
Illustrated by Anthony Lewis

HAMLYN

Contents

First published in Great Britain in 1995 by
Hamlyn Children's Books, an imprint of Reed Children's Books Limited, Michelin House,
81 Fulham Road, London SW3 6RB, and Auckland, Melbourne, Singapore and Toronto.

ISBN 0 600 58551 4

A CIP catalogue record for this book is available at the British Library.

Editor: Veronica Pennycook
Designer: Julia Worth
Consultant: Pat Pye, Ginn & Company Ltd

Printed and bound in Belgium

A New Day

The Sun is up. It's a bright and frosty morning.

Everyone's on the move. Children are making their way to school. Grown-ups leave for work. Even the birds are busy.

4

The Day is Over

Back home in the evening, and the Sun has disappeared. It's dark now. There's time to relax – to play or read, or maybe do nothing at all. It'll soon be bedtime.

Our busy days are followed by quiet nights. Bright days, dark nights – this is the pattern of our lives.

7

Our Home, the Earth

We live on a planet called Earth. Although it seems flat, the Earth is round like a ball. And although it feels still, it's really spinning all the time like a top.

Beyond the Earth, in the darkness of Space, are the Moon, the stars, and the brilliant Sun.

The Bright Sun

Space is as cold and dark as a winter's night. But on Earth we have warmth and light. They come to us from a star – an enormous fireball called the Sun.

The Earth travels right round the Sun during the year. The Sun is fixed in one place; it doesn't move at all.

Sun   Earth

The Sun in the Sky

During the day, the Sun seems to move across the sky. Early in the morning, it rises in the East. By midday, it has climbed high into the sky. In the evening, in a rosy glow, the Sun sets in the West.

Early Morning

West   East

Late Evening

West   East

The Turning Earth

The side of the Earth that faces the Sun has daylight. The other side is dark, and has night. But slowly, as the hours pass, the dark side turns round towards the Sun. The sky grows light. It is morning.

The Earth keeps turning, and the day moves on. Morning changes into afternoon. As the Sun appears to sink in the sky, it is not the Sun that's moving – it's the Earth.

Day

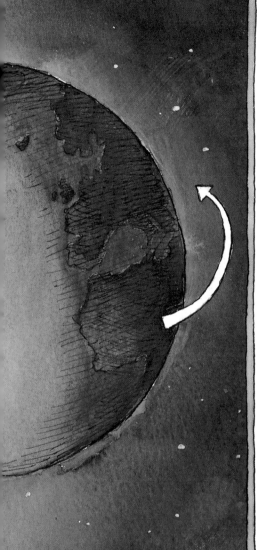

Morning

Turning towards the Sun

Evening

Turning away from the Sun

Imagine you are here

Light and Dark

Our spinning-top Earth takes 24 hours to spin all the way round. While half of the Earth has daylight, the other half has night.

Sweden is about 10,000 kilometres west of Japan. It takes the Earth 6 hours to turn that far. When the Sun is shining in Sweden, it's already dark in Japan!

● **Daytime in Sweden**

Night-time in Japan

What's the Time?

At exactly the same moment, clocks and watches around the world will tell completely different times. It all depends on when it gets light and dark.

At breakfast time in Brazil, the Sun is up, and it's 8 o'clock in the morning. But in Japan, on the other side of the world, the Sun has set, and it's 8 o'clock at night!

Alaska

🕐 1 am

The Night Sky

On a clear night, the sky is a wonderful sight. Millions of stars make pinpricks of light in the darkness. And the bright Moon hangs like a lamp in the sky.

The Moon's shape seems to change. On some nights it's a crescent. On others, it's a circle in the dark sky.

The Changing Moon

The Moon is a big ball of rock that circles the Earth. It has no light of its own. What we call moonlight is really the Sun's light. It shines brightly on one side of the Moon.

The Moon takes 29 days to travel around the Earth, and each night we have a changing view of its sunlit side. Sometimes we see all of it, sometimes just a sliver, and on some dark nights we see no Moon at all.

On the 1st night

● Imagine you are here

What We See From Earth

On the 1st night

After 7 nights

22

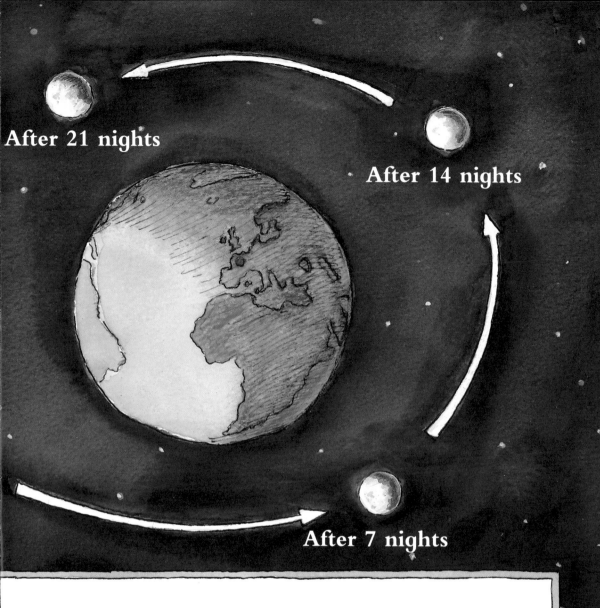

After 21 nights

After 14 nights

After 7 nights

After 14 nights

After 21 nights

Index